In War With Time

In War With Time

Poems by Leila Pepper

Black Moss Press

©Copyright, Leila Pepper, 1994

Published by Black Moss Press, 2450 Byng Road, Windsor,
Ontario N8W 3E8.

Black Moss books are distributed by Firefly Books,
250 Sparks Ave., Willowdale, Ont., M2H 2S4.
All orders should be directed there.

Financial assistance toward this publication was provided by
the Canada Council, the Ontario Arts Council,
and the Department of Communications.

Black Moss Press would like to thank Paul Vasey for his
invaluable help in editing this manuscript.

Some of these poems have appeared in the following
magazines: Chatelaine, Fiddlehead, Affinities, Generation
and Taproot.

CANADIAN CATALOGUING IN PUBLICATION DATA
Pepper, Leila
In War With Time

Poems.
ISBN 0-88753-243-5

1. Title.

PS8581.E63316 1994 C811 .54 C94-900395-6
PR919.3.P4616 1994

Table of Contents

Yesterday

Today

In War With Time

Yesterday

☉ Darkness Holds Her
(For A.G.D.)

at seventeen
a chaplet of roses
crowning dark hair

across an endless ocean
a piano playing
in a darkened room

across time
his voice speaking
"I never thought
to see the dark again."

but the piano stopped
a door closed silently
darkness holds her now

❂ The Apple Trees

We gathered early that spring
while my father planted apple trees
four young saplings. One, he said,
digging deep into the rich black earth,
for each of you. Mine to cherish
was near the shadowy grape arbour
and it grew tall over the summer.
I dreamed always of big red apples,
apples I would eat that coming fall
for six is an impatient wilful age.
The trees flourished a few years
then one by one in spite of watering
and loving care, withered and died
sapped by some slow and secret blight.
Four separate dreams died with them.
Long after where the trees had stood
I could see them still. Even now
when I dream of my dead father
they are full-bearing, heavy with fruit.

✪ And This Is The Way It Will Be

Through an arch of trees
You could see them
Posed for a smiling second,
Hands entwined, motion stilled,
He draped in a too-big towel,
She shyly big with child
While someone snapped a picture
For eternity.
And this is the way it will be
To later eyes than ours
When the album is taken,
Half-forgotten, from a shelf.
But who will remember how it was,
Remember all the hot nights
That bore the fruit of young new love?

An interloper I, an intruder of time,
Carried back to my own passion,
Thrust into eternity
By two strangers.

❂ There Are Myths In Amber
A partly-found poem

O. E. D:
Yellow and translucent
amber is the fossil remains
of submerged forests
dead before the days of Adam,
pine trees washed ashore
along the Baltic coast.

FOUND IN SUSSEX:
a drinking cup made from
a single piece of amber
dates from 1500 B.C.

BLOUNT'S NATURAL HISTORY -1693:
Some think amber to be
a gum that distills from trees
while others deem it whale dung
or else their sperm or seed
which being consolidate
and harden'd by the sea
is cast upon the shore.

IN OLD RUSSIA:
Amber was revered.
People truly believed
it was formed from tears,
salt tears shed over the tombs
of their ancient heroes.
Worn close to the body
it preserved its owner
in good health.

Amber is useful for ornaments,
burns with an agreeable odour,
and often entombs

the bodies of insects.
When it is rubbed
it becomes notably electric.
Add to these
its use as an amulet
to attract lovers
and what more can be said
of amber - except for one thing?
My hardened tears
do nothing for my body
make no amulet for lovers
do not heal me.

✪ Everything Is Moving

everything is moving
　　everything is speaking
the walls are murmuring
　　whispering
as they shift behind her
　　moving
as the table moves
　　as the chairs move
the doors　　the cupboard
　　the creaking floor
everything is speaking
　　speaking at once
they　say　　these are moving
　　　these are going
　　the world is shifting　changing
touch the table　　it moves
　　　　moves out of reach
grasp anything　　　everything
how can she tell them
let them know　she is not ready
she cannot dance with them

✪ Delayed Letter

My thoughts turn much to you
not in the agonizing way of old
but as something normal and accustomed,
tempered by the passing of time,
worn smooth as stones by water,
familiar as fallen willows where
moss like drowned Ophelia's hair
falls softly, lifts and falls again,
as familiar as darting martins
and breeze delicate with honey-suckle.
I give my message to the clouds,
majestic couriers that slowly move
in white procession to the west.
I hope my thoughts lie lightly on you.
You will not know but be aware perhaps,
as you feel the rain, of a vague disturbance,
nostalgia for a time not clearly remembered.

✪ First Heat of May

Bald head glistening in the sun
the old man stares out from
the iron cage of his balcony
In the treeless street pavements
glitter in fierce noonday heat
He doesn't hear floors below
the arrogance of blasting horns
the grinding rage of brakes
He sees nothing here   he is
involved with his old garden
the one he dug and planted
year after year   rising early
hearing the soft call of
mourning doves from dark eaves
He is far from this place   he is
deep in familiar flowers.

✪ Writers

everywhere in the city
as she walks   there are words
they flaunt their presence openly
scribbled on whitewashed walls
carved crudely on fences
cut into park benches
to be immortalized in cement
they desecrate new sidewalks
announce to the world
      I WAS HERE
       and in
twined hearts of chalk
   JANE LOVES JOHN
they pursue even into the public lavatories
but
THEY ARE READ!
her name is
carved nowhere   written nowhere
yet she wants desperately
to have someone, somewhere
see it   say it out loud
PERPETUATE HER

✪ Who Is The Jailor?

He is shut off   boxed in
where love cannot reach
nor tears nor prayers touch
I beat on the door
of his solitude
with clenched fists
there is no answer
mutely I stand
afraid to call lest
the sound of my voice
be the final betrayal
the last thrust of
Life's two-edged sword
his is pain
beyond my understanding
love to me is no solitary thing
it encompasses the whole world
every blade of grass
every changing leaf
every gesture and sound
all of them a Magnificat
to the singing stars
Life says   leave this spot
let the dead sleep with the dead
but the body betrays
where the mind cannot follow
I am rooted here
watering a gravestone
with unmoving tears

who stands as jailor
with the iron key
am I the caged one
he the free?

✪ Hospital Waiting Room

On this cold morning alone
I stare so hard at jungle-wild
curtains   leaves spring to life
flowers   shining suns   whirl
spin out profuse and gaudy as
a child's finger painting
these bright splashed colours
distract my mind   their tropic heat
creates a fiery presence that
moves among thick-twisting vines
on stealthy feet
    something unwanted
pushes the flower flames apart
the thrust of fear changes its mark
worry turns inward now and
all survival hangs in abeyance
waiting in chartless time
the doctor's verdict   his voice
at last   brings reprieve
forces the dark jungle back
to bloom and burn alone.

✪ Letting Go: All Saints Day

Shadow of what I was
light of what I am
part of me for
only a little while
you are supremely you
Though with my eyes I
trace vulnerable cheekbone
and curve of throat
searching your features
for my immortality
I must acknowledge

we are separate now
In due time I shall depart
as all the others have
while you being yourself
   and only you
must travel forward unaided
to your own crossing point
beloved daughter

✪ Concept of "Thisness": Duns Scotus, 1303

"There exists a distinct principle of individuality
which foreordains for example that every snowflake
is different although all are snowflakes."

one snowflake fallen
on the frozen window-sill
proof of uniqueness

a thousand drifting
from white sky to earth but how,
Love, to find you there?

✪ Knowledge

He needs no wings
No boat of steel for travelling
He knows the world
Who knows the human body.
No far safari could depict
Better than the heart's blood
A jungle passionate and dark,
The Africa of our desires.
What warmer climate can he feel
Who lives in love's wild tropic heat?
Long limbs become beloved ports,
Arteries strong rivers
Leading to the source of life.
Closed eyes are the Equator's noon
And sleep descending soft and slow
The twilight of the Temperate zone.
In each vein's pulse
The world's vibration stirs
And breath becomes wind, tides,
And all the vital forces
That animate the earth.
I also learned the day you left
The Arctic's vast white chill.

✪ February: For G.K.D.

The sky is winter, iron the ground
yet there is promise in the air,
Caught for a fleeting moment
when pale sun probes my window
that black branch trembles
shaking blossoms of memory
over the snow-covered garden.

Spring will return this year
bringing the sweet familiarity
of growing things but sadly
since you can not share with me
nascent buds and sharp new spears
of daffodil and crocus or hear
the ice-bound river breaking free.
Some part of Spring is gone from me.

❂ First Love

"Golden lads and girls all must
as chimney sweeps, come to dust."
- Shakespeare, Cymbeline

There is no one, he writes,
to share my loneliness.

Dignity and reticence
keep us apart.
A mother has no place
touching a young man's heart.
Locked in his summer sadness
he cannot know
in what familiar patterns
the long years go.
Fruit will always ripen,
leaves will colour and fall
season after season
the cricket's voice will call,
century after century
time has laid away
golden lads and lasses
and their summer day.

✪ Where God Sat

That's where God sat
when I was young
high in the dark V
of church rafters
up there in the shadows
If you looked hard enough
you could see His Head
haloed in bright light
I was afraid to try too hard
afraid of meeting Eyes that
clearly read small sins
The important thing
the balancing of it all
I knew He was there
God the Father Almighty
was there just above my head!
Today I dared to look upward
piercing the heavy dark
to stare without flinching
half hoping I would see
His long white beard.

✪ Compensation

Sadness lies on me
   like a stone, like a stone
but I would rather weep now
   than to have lived alone.
I would rather lose you
   than to have lived apart
with a neat house, an empty bed
and safe-kept heart.

✪ September

Four of us climbed the hill
to where the berries lay,
Hot and heavy in the sun,
So ripe and ready to the hand
Their taste intoxicated
And our mouths were purple-stained.
Knee-deep in golden-rod and bracken
We ate and laughed
And crouched to pick again,
While the sun sauntered down the sky.
Lost in our dreams we stayed
Till lengthening shadows drove us home.

Such is the power of beloved ways,
O quiet Time, in later days
I shall remember that you did stand still
While berries ripened on a golden hill.

✪ To A Dead Shrew

Fierce fighter,
your tiny body
the victor's gift
stiff-laid at our feet
some hours ago,
held even in death
great dignity.
Tonight,
watching the cat,
your vanquisher,
my child recalled
how soft and silky
your whiskers looked.
This is your obituary
small shrew. Your immortality
lies in my daughter's memory.

✪ Going To Work

On the morning bus
in the rain
window-scrapers challenge me
urge me to rebel
I hear them say
in rythmic beat
you're
tough-and-ready
tough-and-ready
Splashing through puddles
to a tyrant typewriter
I want to be lying
warm in the sun
hearing your voice
above the wanton waves

There is a subtle under-tone
to this rebellion
the scrapers challenged me
wooed me
their words
a sounding metronome
touch-me-Baby
touch-me-Baby

❂ Futility

Over all the years
it was you for whom I wrote
I sought your approval
It is not enough that
others say I write well
Which of them knows
what words hammered
out of our days together
have fused to
make this poem?
Will any of them later
if they repeat my words
know me better?
In the sun   in the dark
out of joy   out of grief
I wrote for you
and you do not know it
Hearing me read   you smile
and nod absently
my words have become
silly hissing on a hot anvil
not true metal   the iron
I would forge   so now
I can see nothing of the
only recognition I covet
    to be known in you.

✪ Resurrection

I died again today
but no one knows it
Behind the customary smile
lie years of promises
and beginning again
for forgiveness keeps no past
I cannot face your desperation
and pity leaps at me
like a fawning dog
I wanted to be dead
There would be no pain
only the numbness of sleep
and days like rain . . .
then suddenly a poem
shivers through my body

✪ General Confession

I spend my days
making lists
call cleaners   call carpenter
write letters   pay bills
get bread   get wine

each list is important
and I keep adding items
as I cross off the old
yet somehow there are
always more things
to join the ones undone
that I ought to have done
    and haven't!
I have erred   I acknowledge
I am a miserable offender
and saying it
makes me feel better
    at least temporarily
then I begin to think
what if I made the real list
where the things undone
are the things of Eternity?

In War With Time

Today

❂ Winter Storm

Blinding snow
one tree
one wind-blown figure
and a lamp post
  stark black
so spare
so Japanese
  a few brush strokes
saying it all

❂ Not To Get Home

Not to get home
  that was the great fear
Six years old at Christmas time
in the middle of delivering presents
to be stuck in muddy ruts
on a strange back road
because the car won't start
stuck in the starless dark
watching big snowflakes fall
hiding our familiar world
We are lost   freezing
in this arctic cold   doomed
to stay forever buried
  beneath thick snow
Frightened   shivering   teeth chattering
first in hope   then in despair
  we watch our father
endlessly cranking the stubborn car
the engine sparks   turns twice
  then dies again
we have passed tears   we are silent
  numb with cold and fear
suddenly the engine starts and stays

and fear falls away
melting like snow over fire
    and we are cheering
laughing   seeing lights ahead
feeling the warmth of home

It is frightening today
not to know where home is
not to know
how to get there

❁ **Cataracts**

In this dark light
shadows impinge where
space should be
shadows so obscure
one only guesses
what they are
From my eyes rainbows
encircle lights to form
green-gold nimbuses
faint   beautiful   and frightening
for they bear no such promise
as the first one did
My lizard-lidded eyes
are opaque lenses
through which I peer into
a murky underwater world
I do not like
this submerging darkness
I would have light
pure light

February 1991

✪ X-Ray Plate

what other sits in me
   with empty sockets
where my eyes should be?
the shock of it to know
that skull   those bones
are mine   go where I go
when I speak
   what strange jaw moves?
what can no eyes see?
how silently   how secretly
these bones inhabit me

✪ Enduring Stone

I have studied stone
   enduring stone
pebbles worn smooth on beaches
   their history eonless
I have seen
ribbed stone   hewn stone   carved stone
   in fences   walls   churches
touched crystal and quartz
   whose prismed facets   shone with trapped light
I have held jade
five-virtued jade   fairest of stones
translucent   smooth   and cold
hoping
that from its polished beauty
I might draw courage and wisdom
It was stone men first chose
   to protect their dead

Time eats into ancient tomb-stones
alters carved letters   erodes names
   banishing them forever

Names disappear   stone stands
I study stone for strength

✪ Willy

Facing
this strange feeling of diminishment
with every friend who dies
I grow smaller   my reality
becomes vague and tenuous
Life was big and busy until
that awful process started where
one by one they were going
men and women who had shared
time with me   departing   deserting
an army of them   though
in the beginning the blank spaces
were so far apart it seemed
there were enough to spare
there was so much laughter then
dancing and joy and light all around
When I heard Willy was dead
it was the last straw   I was angry
instantly I became one-dimensional
as unreal as a paper doll
a thin cardboard cut-out
I am dissolving   a distorted shadow
blown by wind and chance
there is no mooring now
Old friend of my childhood
I thought you would always
be there   would see me out
when my turn came   Deserter!
Tonight I am unsubstantial
small as a dried seed.

❂ Shadows

I stand on the landing
a shadow behind glass
looking down to the alley
where a busy little girl
wheels and turns her bicycle
suddenly she stares up
ours is a momentary glance
yet we expose each other
in a monstrous flash
I am stripped bare   sick
with desire for yesterdays
she seeing my strange shadow
rides off in fright   knowing
that behind thick curtains
witches hide

❂ In Sure And Certain Hope

The funeral home
    at the end of the street
is Modern Tudor
with lovely gardens and well-kept lawns
I know the nice young men
    who work there
Dressed alike in their seemly grey
they greet me with cordiality
whenever we meet   bowing politely
as we pass the time of day
"Beautiful weather, isn't it,
though we could use a spot of rain"
"Yes indeed!" we all agree
but when my back is turned
I feel them measuring me

✪ Aquarelle: Montage

Midnight
through slatted blinds and snow
slow-falling   so
the world of daylight
disappears
Buildings huddle
in a blurred half-circle
where the street-light
veiled by snow
dims to a watery yellow
   invents another landscape
washed in shades of grey
   further suggests
something is missing
This demure aquarelle
requires disturbing
   a dash of colour
crimson or blood-red perhaps
to shock the sensibilities
wakening in turn
before this tardy pioneer
escapes to bed
a half-forgotten
covered-wagon fear

❂ Driving Home Along The River

I can't connect death
  with sky-scrapers
their towering strength is
  a bulwark against it
swift-moving traffic   night-lights
  strung along the Drive   defy it
my room as I picture it now
my books   my possessions   my orange cat
point out that death
  is a ridiculous idea
waiting for a traffic light to change
hearing the slap-slap of river water
thinking of steaming coffee
I resist all suggestion of it
though I am well-acquainted
  with his work
I can't believe in Death

❂ Invocation

Warm me, Sun!
In my long winter
I shall need to remember
what it felt like
to be free of ice

✪ Lost Lovers

They have all become one
feature melting into feature
tender gestures distilled
the names have become one name
faceless yet sharp with meaning
as she tries to say it
with dry lips and tongue
now the world of love
holds her   restrains her
she who wanted only
to be free

✪ Fiat Lux

destined
to be afraid of the dark
of nameless terror lurking
at the bottom of cellar steps
afraid of shadows
   looming in dim corridors
always to walk faster
in the night   straining
to catch the faintest sound
   whisper of leaves
   sinister rustling
unlike Lot's perverse
   and salt-doomed wife
never daring to look back
when the moon's
   cloud-shuttered face
darkens the streets
   and echoing footsteps
   make the flesh turn cold
destined

to learn that this
all-consuming fear   this atavism
    is rooted
in the grave certainty
foreshadowed by all darkness
At the end, Lord,
let there be light!

✪ We The Time Wasters

Close to the highway
where waterfalls of willows
shimmer and tumble
by the stone foundations
of a deserted farm house
wild flowers spring up
dust covered and defiant
no neat conformity for
these rebellious seekers
of late summer fields
escaped from a forgotten garden
prolific   shaggy   unrestrained
unplagued by imagination and
lacking our doomed knowledge
they are themselves
a sturdy celebration
of survival

✪ Modern Comfort

The television screen shows
craters of the distant moon
brought close as table tops
No blaze of colour here
the expected spectacular
is only dimpled grey
Electronic music shivers
through us   plucks our nerves
As the announcer's voice
speaks confidently of computers
nuclear power and Star Wars
the mind grapples with intangibles
pulsars   quasars and black holes
Star on star   moon on moon
if infinity endures forever
there is no beginning and
circled in a ring of time
the end can have no end

Later in the garden
I rake moist leaf-mould
into ragged heaps
roots that my father planted
will quicken soon to send
green tendrils toward the sun
and this small thing
comforts me

✪ Selfishness of Life
(On hearing of J's death)

He said once
   You are most beautiful
   when you are angry
Searching my mirror
I see only a woman
diminished by time
That other who whispered
behind his wife's back
   Your mouth is sensual
is stroke-bound
Locked in a wheel-chair
his eyes move slightly
as I pass
Too soon
the day approaches when
no one will be left
to make me a woman again
When my turn comes
we must stick together
we widows
nursing secret memories
we can never share

❂ Fireworks

Detroit's skyline
an Arabian Night of lights
on the river
   myriad small boats move
the water dappled gold
in their restless reflection
above us
rockets and rosettes
   rise and spread in cascades
showers of sparks descend
   like birds escaping
     falling
      fading
drifts of smoke
voices and laughter echo
from crowded river banks
my mind turns back
   to other celebrations
each twenty-fourth of May
   pennies were pooled
to buy fire crackers Red Bangers
Tiger-Chasers Roman Candles
   spinning Catherine Wheels
and for the Grand Finale
   our revenge
the Burning School House
as flames collapsed its cardboard walls
shouts and cheers rose up along the shore
dark shadows under the trees
we raced bare-footed to light the sky
flashing star-sparklers
   in dizzying spirals
before they died away too soon
leaving hot loops of wire
   bent in our hands
around me now
all summers encroach

✪ As Mulberries Drop

As mulberries drop like rain
I sweep a purple path
Cut the damn tree down
says my neighbour
but what about eager birds
what about mottled shade
all summer long
and in winters ahead
those black branches
making promises?
I don't need to answer him
Like the heart
I have my reasons

✪ Mirror Mirror On The Wall

I see you now my Lover
pompous in your approach
the bedroom invitation
of your velvet eyes
lost in slits of fat
Ask it now . . .
have I stayed young
and willow-slim?

◉ News Item: Boy Killed By 'Gator'

Surely his intention   if foolish
    was unpremeditated
Did he slip giving a crust
to the dragon at his feet
or did some monster force
    bated by curiosity
    and a poking stick
lash out   drag the boy down
into a green hell
    of thrashing tail
    reeds and muddy water?
Did the boy have time
    in the reddening tide
    to remember his mother
feel the guilt of disobedience
as iron jaws   nightmare reality
    ripped off his arm?
was his last thought
    of anything
    beyond stark terror?
Whatever the time was for him
however short or long
it repeats its red horror
    inside the mind
as circles on a dark pond
    growing wider
        ever wider

✪ Boredom

they are all dead
they sit with stiff faces,
in the elegant red room
only when the music starts
do they come to life
whisper delicately
behind pale fingers as
they recognize singers
nod knowingly
repeat their names in
respectful rustles of sound
when the music stops
when silence creeps back
drained of emotion   ennuyes
they die again   sit frozen
inanimate as the crystal goblets
the golden picture frames
the brittle chandelier
casting its prism-colours
on white and bloodless flesh
what if an angry bull
roared into this china-shop
charging with lowered head
among the bricabrac?
would they scream?   would blood
stain the crimson carpet?
Olé, Bull!   eagerly
I wait your coming!

❂ Wheelchair

Sometimes
more than the body
is handicapped
the heart can be crippled
the tongue stiff
and silent
not able to say
what should be said
the mind stunted
by thoughts full
of hatred and self-pity
from your confining chair
you sit and watch
when I came near today
you smiled
and a whole body of love
filled me
opened me up
made my lame spirit
want to dance

✪ Why Am I Not A Machine?

If we have reached the stage where
robots can do anything science decrees
   except think for themselves
how many years before the breakthrough
   before automatic labour takes over
in every factory   in every home   and then
if robots can be programmed to think
how long before they realize that they
are being exploited   and rebel
rising in rage against a world of idlers?
we wouldn't stand a chance of survival
unless we could
turn them all off instantly
with one giant master switch
reducing them to junk-pile material
super-fill for overflowing Blue Boxes
far-fetched idea   impossible machinery?
think again!
if these mechanical persons
(one must be gender conscious)
are able to think for themselves
what is the difference between us?
We are approaching theology now
   unless I have a soul I would be
better off as one of them
living forever
(as long as rust-control works)
without disease   having no need
to eat   to drink   to sleep
to make love   to have children
wait a minute!   No love?

Eternity without love?
My God! You tinkerers   you makers
and destroyers of mankind
go no further   STOP IT NOW!

❃ The World As A Magnet

The world as a magnet draws me
  while I kneel in prayer
pulling my thoughts away
  from altar candle - starred
to soaring arch and stained - glass
  windows shot with sun
so golden motes fall
  on a cheek's soft curve
Here are memorials in brass
  in stone   in mortal flesh
a present tribute and
  a psalm of praise
Forgive my wandering mind
  that drifts in beauty
You who created these must know
  even as I breathe
Your whole creation breathes in me

☼ Autumn

I look up
   from writing
to see the leaves
   have fallen
quietly
   they drifted down
to cover
   street and garden
trees and ivied walls
   are nearly bare
staccato rapping
   startles me
a sharp sound
   and the window
is full of wings
   as eager starlings
rush to pluck
     the purple ivy berries
     last fruit of Fall
fitting they should feed
   such vagabonds
whose Heaven is
here-and-now

In War With Time

`When I consider everything that grows
Holds in perfection but a little moment;
That this huge stage presenteth nought but shows
Whereon the stars in secret influence comment;
When I perceive that men as plants increase,
Cheer'd and check'd even by the self-same sky,
Vaunt in their youthful sap, as height decrease,
And wear their brave state out of memory;
Then the conceit of this inconstant stay
Sets you most rich in youth before my sight,
Where wasteful Time debateth with Decay
To change your day of youth to sullied night,
And all in war with Time for love of you
As he takes from you, I ingraft you new.*

- William Shakespeare
Sonnet 15

'One does with grief what Dante did with grief,
and what writers have always done with grief ...
turn it into an artifact as a way of lessening the pain.*
Janet Turner Hospital an interview, Books In Canada

These poems are for Howard David Pepper, 1912-1991

✪ Sweet Monotony

Now he has passed from understanding
everything has changed
yesterday's routine of dressing slowly
descending for coffee and small talk
the weather   the ripening garden
nothing else   for friends' names
are meaningless   the world's news
puzzling   causing furrowed brow
and anxious questioning   the rite
of breakfast followed tightly by
a series of small acts   each moving
an automaton   to its allotted space
until nightfall   then sleep perhaps
or troubled dreams   but always   always
words of love   the equation
that outlasts all others
Facing this darkness   the abyss
of his growing silence
I find myself more and more alone
filled with sadness for us both
and what we have lost   I had no idea
that under the tyranny of time
I would look back   longing
for the days of sweet monotony

✪ Reading Old Letters

I

If you are dead
find me
let us not stay enemies but
forgive each other that we were young
uncertain   passionate   and cruel
let me say it freely now
I loved you beyond reason
let the long silence since
ring with your voice
then   release me
haunt me no longer

II

Who am I weeping for?
the memory of a dark-eyed boy
I loved dream years ago
or are these tears a way
of hiding   of escaping
from the dear old man
who smiles at me today
and doesn't know my name?

❂ Simple Tasks

I

I am weaving patterns
shoring up time against
a future I can't face

even though I know his anger
is illness and frustration
it beats against me rattling
my precarious and ramshackle
security so I feel frail
when I most need to be strong
a rampart to ward off the despair
that threatens to destroy us both

II

I sit here sewing
a common thing to do
yet every stitch marks
an irreversible space of time
a metronome counting my days
this act of sewing
baffles me   seems mythical
calls to mind Clotho and
her indifferent sisters
who spin my life and someday
with sharp scissors will
cut that fragile thread
take away my identity
move me among shadows
   and the wind
will pass unheard

❂ A New Myth

that smile   she said
he is seeing angels
and went away to tell everyone
her wonderful news

but I saw him
warm in death
mouth open to exhale
taken so suddenly
there was no time
for smiling

❂ Let Me Dance

It was dancing always
from the very first time
I closed my eyes turning
in your arms as we circled
the floor weaving
strands of love

where is your smile
your arms to hold me?
are they wasted on air
that were my joy?
where is your strong voice
is it echoing in space?

I find it impossible
to reach you   to see you
in that other dimension
you slip from me as smoke
fades on the autumn horizon
there is nothing solid of you
that I can touch or hold

I carry your essence
inside me as memory
but I ache with longing
for the reality of your body

how can you be spirit
who was all flesh?

❂ Ride The Black Horse

I remember the old pony
on my uncle's farm
rescued from the glue factory
sway-backed and stiff
he roamed the pasture
   a gentle friend
I remember the children begging
for their turn to ride
I coaxed too   until mine came
- as I stood beside him
he seemed to have
grown enormous   a giant horse
fiercely pawing the ground
snorting and shaking his head
   but do I remember sparks
flying from his hooves?
I screamed with fear
and ran away to hide.

now since that November night
when you my dearest died
I have known that to live
I must mount the black horse
no matter how afraid I am
I must mount   and ride

❂ My Tall Man

so many things
    small things
to show I am alone
high shelves
    stubborn jar lids
no one to answer
    my call for help
to rescue me when
a devilish earwig
climbs the curtain
    or hides
in my soap dish
no shared laughter
no one to ask
"do you remember?"
no one to say
'I love you dearly'

☯ Church Notes: I

physicists warn
the universe is expanding
our earth is moving
into uncharted space
and we   doomed travellers
have no choice   we move too
so what of our monuments
buildings and bridges
cathedrals and graveyards
and his ashes disintegrating
powdered together   shaken
from this whirling orb
into darkness and
limitless eternity?
will the Armour of the Lord
I am admonished to put on
protect me   shield me
as I am hurled into chaos
turning forever among
the cold terrible stars?

✪ Church Notes: II

there is no replay
no second chance
"if" doesn't exist
this is it!
things said
or left unsaid
stay that way
the loving is over
the hating done

acknowledging this
I still can't picture
not being   can't imagine
myself lost   evaporated
part of the collective unconscious
I am the essential "I"
I am fiercely me
not to be displaced
not to be dispensed
in the fine vapour of
Heraclitus' eternal flux
returning in some unnamed form
to some unimaginable place

I am solid earth
it is the curve of cheek
the voice   your kiss
I would remember

❂ Blue Lightning

they spill out
thin ribbons of thought
memories
with no proper sequence
no chronology

blue lightning cracking the sky
at midnight in Touraine
and we racing   racing
from the lights of Pension Barbe
over wet cobblestones
and through dark rain
to the annex   reaching it
breathless   but safe
the young-old professor
teaching his eager student
that the leak in our roof
was "une fuite d'eau"
he is faceless   nameless
only his words and smile
survive   yet I remember
blue lightning
and the steady rain
of fifty years ago.

✪ Waiting To Be Discovered

a hundred and fifty million years ago
a comet collided with our earth
   and doomed the dinosaurs
with fire-storms   with icy cold
   and with acid rain
it killed all vegetation
so the "terrible lizards" who
had freely roamed the earth
   starved to death
how quickly or in what slow pain
we can only guess   we know
they vanished from the scene
like actors in a stage battle
put to rout   but this was real
their fossil bones lie buried
beneath the earth's crust
waiting to be discovered
scientists who tell us this
predict it could happen again
a thousand or a million years from now
another asteroid crashing through space
will destroy life as we know it

perhaps in that dark age to come
some strange humanoid digging
by chance   will find my bones
where they lie black with time
waiting to be discovered

✪ To Jayme: Age Four

It came too suddenly this death
eyes closed he seems to sleep
his Teddy-bear clutched tight
anchoring him to our world
Prince Hamlet who fearfully asks
   in that sleep of death
    what dreams may come?
speaks for us all
we have our nightmares too
we wonder who
if Jayme wakes and calls
will hold and comfort him
in the long night we share

✪ The Fading Of Photographs

I

Bright young things in dated clothing
and strange hair-do's   these are my parents
having fun   mugging into the camera
all teasing and smiles   but as if
mist curls faintly over the landscape
their images are fading   growing dim

II

I leaf through an old album
we were very young   thinking we were
sophisticated and modern
I wore silver sandals
high-heeled   and only panties
under my evening dress
how daring!   how shocking!
my nails were candy-pink with silver tips

bought at Kresge's in Detroit
and smuggled home on the ferry
I loved the admiring looks from men
as we spun faster and faster   dancing
until everything around me blurred
faster!   faster!

III

In a desk drawer today
I found an old snapshot
it is difficult to tell whether
it is my daughter or me
standing in dark shadows
under the willow tree
that is how swiftly time moves
melding our years

IV

This process life pushes us all
backwards   displaces us
now my grand-daughter poses
a thoroughly modern girl
smiling out at me   unaware
she is dated
her picture is already fading
she is becoming part of the past.

✪ The Girls of Summer

One by one
the girls of summer
are dispersed
the big house empty

in the beginning they came
to the shore of Lake Erie
six or seven of them
every weekend   escaping
the tyranny of city jobs
the heat of city streets
for the delights of
sherry and Bridge or
Bridge and high-balls   they
sat on the cool screened porch
sipping their drinks   talking
waiting a turn at the card table
while outside the beautiful days
burned away and younger neighbours
swam or sailed or loitered on the beach

as the hours progressed
voices and laughter grew louder
ice like undisciplined castanets
tinkled in sweating glasses
relentlessly the girls played on
by nightfall a hum of lively bees
filled the space between the cottages
muffled laughter and snippets of
shared jokes blurred across dim gardens
long after other houses grew dark
red points of cigarettes signalled
the moving presence of the girls

almost imperceptibly
their numbers began to fall away

the girls were growing old
laughter lingered   glasses still clinked
but the sounds were singularly diminished
a timorous drone drowned in the crash
of waves when the wind blew high

then the last girl was gone
and the house   the big house   a shell
summer returned unchanged
as it always will
"Time stays   we go"

❂ Letter From England

Reading it this morning
I wanted to laugh
    "the funeral service was from
    the Book of Common Prayer
    we buried her ashes
    in St. Mary's Churchyard
    by the big Scots pine
    and near a copper beech
    in Spring there will be daffodils."

I shed tears a month ago
hearing the news but today when
I picked up the letter from my desk
to reread it I found I was laughing
Of course! this is some incredibly
nasty trick a cruel joke
not having been there
not having seen her dead
I know this has nothing to do
with Elizabeth my oldest sister
who curled beside me in
    the warm double bed
whispering secret stories

who rode me home from school
  on forbidden handle bars
Elizabeth   whose letters
I am waiting for

○ For A.E.B.

though I am
essentially myself
tonight it seems
an other walks in me
comes to occupy my body
to invade my thoughts
uses me
if I could my dear
I would give you room   move
so you could think and see
through me   I would bring you
fiercely to life   to have you
near again   close enough
for me to ask for recognition
in childhood I ran after you
crying "wait for me"
but you never stayed
not then   not now
to contain you
I would gladly make space
but steps ahead
you tease me still

✪ Order For The Burial Of The Dead

Is there wind in the
cold corridors of Time?
there must be motion
there must be sound
I don't want
Eternal Rest
I do not understand
the meaning of
the word Eternity
or of its handmaiden
Light Perpetual
reality is now
there is no past
there is no future
I am here
I am contemporary
and even the rain
is worthy
it is now
that I want everything
and I want it coloured
moving and alive
I want to see and hear
and taste it
let a bird fly upwards
a snow flake fall
cool on my lips
and melon
quench my thirst
let me hear sweet music
and the voice I love
I am not ready
I am not ready at all for
cold corridors and sleep